The Story of Christmas

Told in pictures by Margaret Tarrant
and in simple words by Katharine Bamfield

LONDON: THE MEDICI SOCIETY LTD.

This edition published in 2024 by Arcturus Publishing Limited
26/27 Bickels Yard, 151–153 Bermondsey Street,
London SE1 3HA

First published in 1952

Author: Katherine Bamfield
Illustrator: Margaret Tarrant

For this Arcturus edition:
Editor: Becca Clunes
Designer: Allie Oldfield
Design Manager: Jessica Holliland
Managing Editor: Joe Harris

ISBN: 978-1-3988-3971-7
CH006523UK
Supplier 29, Date 0624, Print run 00005992

Printed in China

The Story of Christmas

God's Promise of a Saviour

The Bible tells us that in the Beginning God created Man in His own Image. But very soon men and women began to do the things God had told them not to do, and with their disobedience sin came into the beautiful world that God had made. God was very sorry and He pitied mankind and made a promise that in His own time He would send a Saviour to help them.

For hundreds of years God's people wondered when His promise was coming true, for all the time the hope of a Messiah or Deliverer was kept alive in their hearts by the Prophets who were teachers chosen by God. But most people were looking for a powerful earthly King, who would lead his armies into battle and make their nation free and great.

At last, at God's appointed hour, an Angel—Gabriel who stands in the presence of God—was sent to earth to carry the joyful news that the Time had come, the promised Deliverer was to be born, as the Prophets had foretold.

Now the Angel's message was not given to a Princess or a great lady, but to Mary of Nazareth, a humble maiden, who was about to marry Joseph, the carpenter. But though Joseph was only a carpenter by trade, the great King David was his ancestor, and prophets of old had all promised that the coming Messiah or Saviour should be of the royal line of David.

Mary was overcome by the Angel's tidings—that she was to be the Mother of the Holy One, the Son of God. But she answered the call in simple and humble obedience.

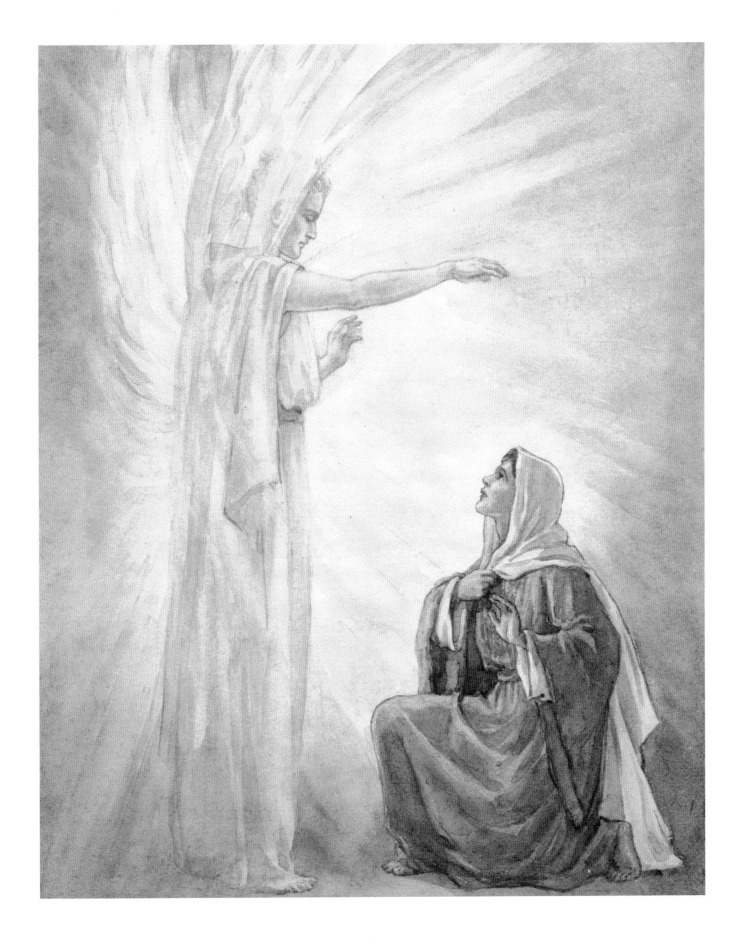

The Angel messenger

Gabriel had also spoken to Mary of her cousin Elizabeth, for she too was to be the mother of a promised son, known to us as St. John the Baptist. He was to prepare the way for one greater than himself—Mary's own Son.

Just before the time came for Mary's babe to be born into the world, the Roman Emperor ordered all his subjects to report at the place where they belonged, so that his officers might count the number of people. So Joseph and Mary had to set out for Bethlehem, the City of David, the very place where the Prophets had said the Messiah should be born.

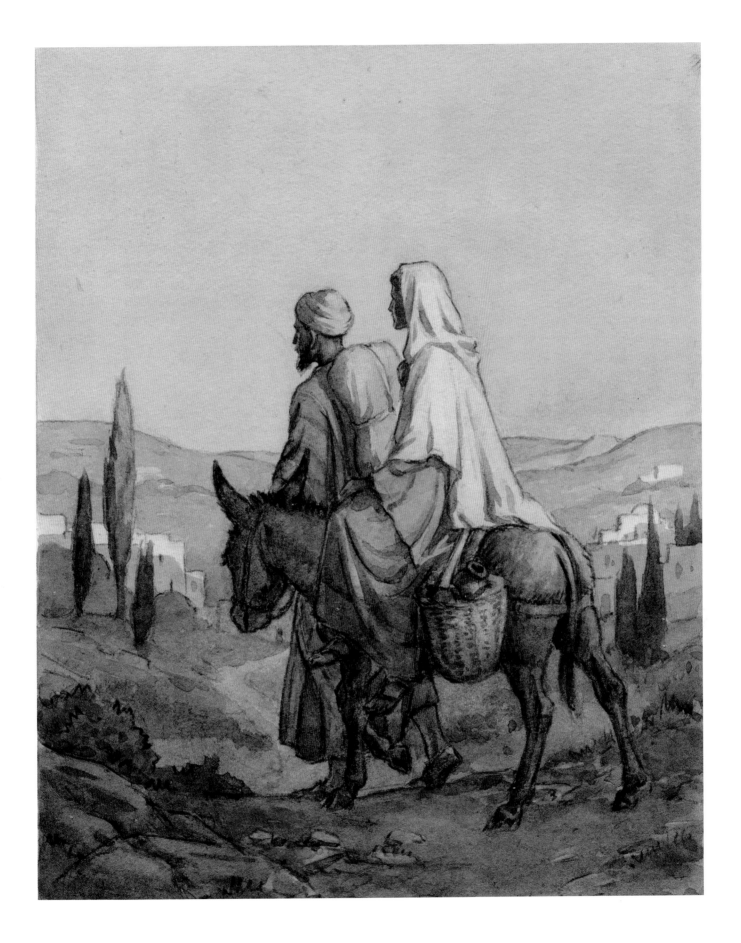

Mary and Joseph on the road to Bethlehem

There were great crowds moving about, for many were travelling because of this census, or counting of the people, and when Joseph and Mary got to Bethlehem the Inn was full. So they had to shelter in the stable, and there, in that humble place, Mary's Babe was born. He was the Heavenly King, the son of God, but He had no earthly place, not even a real bed, and His mother laid Him to sleep in a manger.

The newborn Saviour

Men did not know who had come to live among them, but the Angels were watching, and they told the wonderful news to some simple Shepherds, as they guarded their sheep in the fields that night.

And the rejoicing of Heaven overflowed unto earth as the Angel hosts sang together "Glory to God in the Highest and on earth Peace, Goodwill towards men."

Then the Shepherds thought they would go and see their newborn Saviour for themselves, for had not the Angel said "Unto you is born a Saviour"?

The Angel appears to the Shepherds

And they left their flocks and walked to Bethlehem as fast as they could in the night. When they got to Bethlehem they found it was all true, just as the Angel had told them.

There was the newborn Babe and His Mother and Joseph. And the Baby was lying in the manger that held hay for the oxen to eat. But the Shepherds knew this was no ordinary infant. And they worshipped Him.

Eight days after His birth

the baby Boy received His Name

as an Angel had foretold to Joseph.

Note that Name and what it means. JESUS—

"for He shall save His people from their sins."

The Shepherds nearing Bethlehem

The Shepherds arrive

The Stable at Bethlehem

Later on, forty days from His birth, Mary and Joseph took Him to the Temple to be presented and dedicated to the Lord, and there a wonderful thing happened. A very old and holy man named Simeon had been assured by the Holy Spirit that he should see "the Lord's Christ" before he died. Coming into the Temple just then he felt that promise to him was being fulfilled. Taking the Child in his arms, he knew that here lay the Saviour, not only of Israel, but of the whole world.

"Mine eyes have seen Thy Salvation, which Thou hast prepared before the face of all people," sang Simeon, and his words still ring out in Christian worship every day at evening.

The Presentation

Then appeared three magnificent figures—Wise Men (or Magi) from the East. They had seen a new star, a royal star—the sign of a King—appear in the eastern sky. Guided by its light they set out on a long journey to find this new monarch. The star pointed to Jerusalem, and when they arrived there they enquired of King Herod where the new King was to be born. "At Bethlehem" answered the priests, who knew what was written in the sacred books.

And at Bethlehem, still led by the Star, the Magi found the infant King. (By this time the holy Family had moved into a house, and the little Lord Jesus no longer lay in a manger.) The travellers entered into His presence and fell down and worshipped Him. Then they opened the treasures they had brought and laid them at His feet.

The Magi approach Bethlehem

The gifts that St. Matthew's gospel mentions have, no doubt, a spiritual meaning. They offered Gold to Him as King, with Frankincense they worshipped Him, and they laid bitter Myrrh before him as a token of His sufferings yet to come.

When the Magi had enquired of King Herod about this new king, Herod pretended that he too wished to pay homage to the unknown monarch, but really he was jealous at the idea of a rival, and made up his mind to kill Him.

The Wise Men did not visit Herod again, as he had asked them to do, for God gave them a warning in a dream, and they returned to their own country by another way.

An Angel warned Joseph in a dream of Herod's wicked intention and told him to take Mary and the holy Child and to escape into the land of Egypt.

The Magi offer their gifts to Jesus

They stayed in Egypt as long as Herod lived, and when they returned to their own country, it was in Nazareth that they settled, a safer spot than Bethlehem, as Herod's son was reigning in his father's place.

And the name of Nazareth is for ever sacred to us, as it was the home of the Lord Jesus in His boyhood.

There Joseph the carpenter had his workshop. There Jesus "wrought with Joseph with chisel, saw and plane." In that home

Jesus in the carpenter's shop

He was "subject to His parents" and obeyed them, and there He "increased in wisdom and stature and in favour with God and man."

The story of Christmas is ended. But it never grows stale or out of date. To all who hold out loving hands of welcome to the Christ Child, and kneel at His cradle, He bestows a gift that lasts for ever—even a share in His own divine eternal Life.